STEP PARENTS

The Essential Guide

Samantha
Harrington-Lowe

Step-Parents – The Essential Guide is also available in accessible formats for people with any degree of visual impairment. The large print edition and e-Book (with accessibility features enabled) are available from Need2Know. Please let us know if there are any special features you require and we will do our best to accommodate your needs.

First published in Great Britain in 2012 by
Need2Know
Remus House
Coltsfoot Drive
Peterborough
PE2 9BF
Telephone 01733 898103
Fax 01733 313524
www.need2knowbooks.co.uk

Contents

Introduction

These days it can often feel like a 'normal' nuclear family is something of a rarity; that most families are varied, broken up or diverse. Children find themselves with step-parents, half-siblings, or living in single-parent households – even having same-sex parents. It's a time when the family unit is a much more flexible arrangement, rather than the biological 'Mum, Dad and their biological children' configuration of the past.

The most common structure away from the traditional is that of two families coming together, creating step-parents and step or half-siblings and therefore a whole new family; and this book looks at how parents can build a stepfamily successfully, offering advice, support and guidance

Having step-parents and siblings can be a fulfilling and rewarding experience, creating a loving and thriving family home. Hundreds of thousands of diverse family structures exist successfully, offering support and happiness to children and parents alike. But it's not always easy – there can be many challenges along the way and it's fair to say that often, making a stepfamily work requires a fair bit of effort. It can be fraught with difficulties; with resentment, resistance, incompatibility, arguments about money, issues with other parents . . . there are plenty of ways this new arrangement can offer complications. But all families take work, and stepfamilies are no different. It's just a more complex set of problems.

The variations for the stepfamily set-up and the problems and challenges associated with it are too many and too complex to be addressed in one small book, and it's impossible to try and cover everything. Therefore, what you read here may not directly address your own situation, but we have tried to give a broad overview, and this book should help you understand some of the challenges associated with blended families, and developing new coping mechanisms and strategies to deal with them.

'Having step-parents and siblings can be a fulfilling and rewarding experience, creating a loving and thriving family home.'

Chapter One

What is a Stepfamily?

What is a stepfamily?

Technically, a stepfamily is one where the two adult partners are married or cohabiting, as is increasingly the case, and have come into the relationship with children of their own who have other parents. Marriage used to be the defining characterisation, but living together creates the same structure, even if the children also spend time with their other parents. It's about sharing living space, about creating a family home. Adults may refer to their partner's child as their stepson or daughter even if they still live full-time with their other parent, but this is unusual – a stepfamily is normally one that lives under the same roof, whether full-time or part-time, married or cohabiting.

The difference between step-siblings and half-siblings

There's a big difference between steps and halves. This is all about shared parents – stepbrothers and sisters will have no blood relatives between them; the only reason they're in the same family is because of marriage or cohabitation. Half brothers and sisters share one parent.

Let's take an example – Bob and Annette get married. Bob has a son, Peter, and Annette has a daughter, Sabrina. Sabrina and Peter both have other parents so they are simply stepbrother and sister to each other.

If Bob and Annette have a child together, Stephen, Stephen shares a father with Peter and a mother with Sabrina – therefore he is their half brother.

Parental responsibility

Legal rights of step-parents

As a step-parent it's good to know where you stand legally, and although married or living together, parental responsibility still rests with one or both of a child's natural parents, provided they are both named on the birth certificate. The Children Act 1989 defines parental responsibility as 'All the rights, duties, powers, responsibilities and authority which by law a parent of a child has in relation to the child and his property'.

There are many step-parents who would like parental responsibility for the child or children they are raising, and there are ways to achieve this; through adoption, a parental responsibility order, a residence order or special guardianship.

Before starting down any of these lines, remember that whatever it is that you want from this relationship, the most important person in this decision process is the child. Think carefully about your course of action, and make sure it's in the child's best interest, not just because it's something you want to do for yourself.

'As a step-parent it's good to know where you stand legally, and although married or living together, parental responsibility still rests with one or both of a child's natural parents, provided they are both named on the birth certificate.'

Adopting stepchildren

Step-parents can become legal parents of their partner's children through adoption. If you're planning to adopt your partner's child or children, and their other parent is alive and has parental responsibility, you will need their permission, and you will need to apply to your local council three months before starting proceedings. There are cases where the courts may override this need for permission – if the other parent is abusive, for example, or has been harmful or neglectful – but these cases need to be fairly extreme and largely you will need to make an agreement with the child's other parent. Not paying maintenance, for example, is not admissible, nor is absenteeism. Their permission will still need to be sought.

Need2Know

If the child's parent is hard to contact, the court will expect you to advertise to try and find that parent. Adoption will end the natural parent's parental responsibility so legal advice should be sought by all parties before proceeding with this.

Adoption is for life and it's good to think very carefully about this as a choice. There will be involvement and visits from social services, and court appearances. And from the child's perspective it could be very unsettling. Remember, should you wish to adopt your partner's child and that child has not seen their other parent for some time, the adoption procedure may well inevitably rekindle contact with them through the process – is that something you want? Is the child settled? Do they need that disruption? It will also affect wider family – will that child want to lose their natural parent's own mother and father as their grandparents? Because legally, that is a consequence. Look at all the angles of adoption and ensure it's the right thing for the child.

Parental Responsibility Agreement

A step-parent and natural parent married to each other or living together may apply for a Parental Responsibility Agreement. This is a fairly straightforward form-filling exercise witnessed by the courts that means both natural parents and the step-parent share parental responsibility. It does not involve social services and can be fast to set up, and suggests a good working relationship between all adult parties caring for the child or children. The agreement lasts until the child is 18.

Parental Responsibility Order

Should the other parent oppose a Parental Responsibility Agreement you can apply for a Parental Responsibility Order. The outcome of this application is decided by the courts and may well be part of other proceedings relating to the child. It is often more complicated and may involve social services or court appearances.

'Adoption is for life and it's good to think very carefully about this as a choice.'

Residence order

This is an order stating that the child lives with the person who has the order, and it also means that that person or persons have parental responsibility for that child. This can work well if the child lives with you, but parental responsibility only applies if the child is living with you. The drawback for a step-parent is that the order only applies when the child is living with him or her, so, for example, if the step-parent and birth parent separated with the step-parent moving out, the step-parent would then lose parental responsibility.

Overseas procedures

If applying for any of the above orders or rights and the child's parent is overseas or a foreign national the application procedures are the same but you may find that the rules in the other country are different from the UK, and it may also take much longer. Ensure you engage the legal services of counsel who understand intercountry adoption or parental responsibility procedures and prepare for a tough challenge.

Summing Up

- More than any of the legal applications we've talked about, or what type of set-up your family is, the most important thing to consider when setting up a stepfamily is creating a loving family home. Children need love, continuity, stability and support. Don't go into this lightly, make sure it's something you really want, that you think will last.

- Be prepared to have your preconceptions challenged – the picture you have in your head of the happy family home may be very different from the reality! Children form attachments very early on to their natural parents and adapting to Mum or Dad's new husband or wife could be tricky for them – and for you. But all families take work and a stepfamily is no different.

- With input and commitment, there is no reason why your stepfamily shouldn't be happy, successful and rewarding for all.

Chapter Two

The Children

Meeting your future stepchildren for the first time

So this is it! You've met the love of your life, the person of your dreams and it's the most perfect relationship you've ever had – everything works and you've never been so happy. The future looks bright, and you plan to spend the rest of your lives together.

Well okay, so maybe that's jumping ahead a little – the chances are that when you meet your future stepchildren for the first time, you'll be meeting them simply as the child or children of your new partner. It's unlikely, although possible, that you've been introduced as their new step-parent. It takes time before that usually becomes apparent and many new partners will hold off introducing their children to new lovers until they are sure it's going to be ongoing and serious. After all, whilst it's realistic for children to understand that sometimes Mum and Dad won't be together and it's okay for them to have other partners, nobody needs a trail of short-term 'uncles' or 'aunts' through their lives.

So the first time you meet them could be fairly casual. It's likely that you're both going to be wary – there could be jealousy or resentment as the child or children feel they may have competition for their parent's attention. You too may feel threatened. It's important to remember that, as with any relationship, things take time. Take it gently, remember who the adult is and try not to get drawn into any animosity if it's there. Take an interest in the child but don't overdo it, trying too hard . . . children can spot that a mile off! Once the

> 'Take it gently, remember who the adult is and try not to get drawn into any animosity if it's there.'

relationship is clearly stable and it's apparent you're all going to be making a family life together, laying the foundations of kindness and dignity at this stage will pay dividends in the future.

Introducing step-siblings to each other

Again, this is something that is unlikely to happen as a 'fait accompli'. In other words, you're unlikely to be introducing your children to each other with the words, 'Meet your new stepbrother/sister.' You're far more likely to have all spent time together before coming together as a stepfamily, getting to know each other, spending time doing activities and eating together . . . if good relationships can be built up during this phase, it will again support a more intense family structure later in the future.

'It's very common for children to feel an intense rush of loyalty for the other parent at a time when two new partners come together.'

If your children all take an instant dislike to each other, it's going to be harder work. Just remember, Rome wasn't built in a day, and the children will be experiencing a very complex set of emotions. Resentment, fear, insecurity – all these will come into play as a child feels their home life to be threatened and disrupted. Children resist change, and will naturally be afraid their parent is being drawn away from them. The appearance of someone else's children in their parent's life is going to be hard. Be patient. Ensure you spend quality time with your own children away from the new relationship so they know you're still there for them. But make a point of being clear about your intentions if you can – children know when something's up and whilst you must reassure them that they are still your key focus and you love them very much, it's also important for them to understand that you too need love. As with all these things, communication is the key.

Understanding roles

Ensuring stepchildren know you're not replacing the role of their natural parent

It's very common for children to feel an intense rush of loyalty for the other parent at a time when two new partners come together. If a child has spent many years growing up with Mum and Dad, that child will not only struggle with the separation, but will often really resent the incoming new step-parent. The same for children who may not have spent that time in a nuclear family. They could be terrified that their mother or father is being replaced.

On a more complex level, it could be that the absent mum or dad is in fact something of a letdown – for example perhaps they are an unfit parent, or just not around very much, or abusive. In situations like this, conversely, the resentment can be even stronger. Far from welcoming a new step-parent who could perhaps do the job properly, the child may feel the other parent's shortcomings even more acutely, and resent the step-parent for being better than their own.

Getting to know the child

What works well in all these situations is developing your own relationship with the child. It's not the same as being their mum or dad, it's a different role, and by working with the child or children directly, rather than being Mum or Dad's girlfriend or boyfriend, you will find that your own relationship will develop naturally. Explain to them that you don't want to be new Mum or Dad and that you wouldn't want to replace them. Spend time with them away from your partner and get to know them on your own level. Keep at it, and they will come to understand that it's okay to have another, new type of relationship with you and that you're not a direct substitute.

Balancing discipline and friendship

The above notwithstanding, it's important to find a respectful balance. It's easier when children are a bit younger to strike this balance with a bit more ease, but taking on teenage children, for example, can be tough. There's a fine line here and it's something that you and your partner should discuss too – where the boundaries lie, for example. It's no good you drawing a line in the sand over something if your partner is going to overrule it or vice versa. Children will pick up their cue from the way the two of you work the parenting job together so ensure you have a united front. Consider what you'd like the children to call you, and be aware that being able to discipline them goes hand in hand with putting in some of the good energy too. You can't go telling them off all the time without giving them some quality time and input on other levels.

Telling the children that you may marry, or live together

How you tell the children that you are moving in together or getting married will largely be driven by how well you think they're going to take it. It might be that everyone is going to be excited about this possibility and looking forward to the whole adventure, it might be that the children are very small and won't really understand what's going on. But it could equally be that you have one or two sets of children who absolutely hate the idea; in which case your job is going to be much harder!

Talking to them, as with everything, is going to be the key. If they're small, focus on the things that matter to small children, such as what kind of bedroom they're going to have, how their daily routine will be affected. With younger children it's the immediacy of how life will operate that will be the issue. With older children, it's important to stress that they hold a special place in this shared household, and that they'll still get time with their own parents as well as together as a family. Talk it through together to see what everyone expects from the home set-up and as far as is reasonably possible, ensure everyone has a voice in how the household is run.

If there is a child who might not be at the house full-time, it's just as important to make that child feel they have an equal stake in the space or relationship. He or she should still have their own room if everyone else has, and it's vital that when they do stay with you, they feel part of the family, not like a visitor.

Moving in together is a big step and you should be prepared for the possibility of a bumpy ride! But children who are difficult are usually difficult for a reason – they're hurt or afraid or insecure. Time will make a huge difference and, as with balancing discipline and friendship in the relationship with your stepchildren, it's vital that you and your partner talk this through and agree a strategy together before dealing with the children

'How you tell the children that you are moving in together or getting married will largely be driven by how well you think they're going to take it.'

Understanding children if you have none of your own

How do children work?

Ah, if only they came with a handbook! Children are complex and complicated creatures and it's impossible to explain how they work in anything less than a book the size of Big Ben! But there are a few key things to look out for that will help and guide you.

Children have a few basic needs that need fulfilling in order to help them work properly. They need to be able to feel safe – to know the environment they exist in will support them, whatever happens. They need to feel able to form attachments to people, whether it's parents, step-parents, grandparents or friends, and be able to trust in that attachment. If children are being difficult, there's a reason for it. It could simply be that they're struggling with a new family coming together, problems with their other parent, difficulties at school or with peers, perhaps they're being bullied. But bad behaviour should be seen as a symptom. Children are not 'born bad'.

It might sound crazy but simple support structures for children will work wonders. A good night's sleep, decent healthy food, quality time with parents and a voice that can be heard in a family will all help. Listen to them, talk to them, spend fun time with them and show a genuine interest in their lives – all this will help. They need to feel valued and loved and supported. A bit of common sense will go a long way.

'If you're taking on a partner with children and you have none of your own, there's absolutely nothing wrong with feeling daunted or afraid of failure.'

Getting some help

If you're taking on a partner with children and you have none of your own, there's absolutely nothing wrong with feeling daunted or afraid of failure. Children don't really come with a 'How-to' manual, and all kids are different.

Chat to other family members perhaps. Do you have siblings who have children? Or friends? Think of it as a new job that you need to research a bit and don't be afraid to ask for help. You'll find that even parents who have been in the job for years still don't have all the answers! The library will have a huge section on parenting, or there are numerous websites you can look through.

Respect and disrespect

Dealing with disrespect and not taking things to heart

It's common, particularly with older children, for them to be resentful and disrespectful towards a step-parent. It's a tough one this, as it can really rock a household and certainly doesn't set a good example for other children in the house. It's hard to stay calm if you have a child shouting back at you, refusing to respond to discipline or boundaries, ignoring requests, being rude and insolent.

At the heart of these issues, again, is the importance of having a clear strategy with your partner. Whether it's your child or theirs causing the issue, it's important to decide together how you will cope with this.

Firstly, it's really important to understand that you need to build a relationship with your stepchild or children before attempting to discipline them. They will respond much better to someone they love and trust, so during the early days, aside from day-to-day routine, leave the discipline to the biological parent.

Responding with anger can be hard to avoid but it's best to try and do so, and you should talk to the child together, let them know this is not acceptable behaviour, and lay down some ground rules from the start. Use diversionary tools to take control of the situation and don't let yourself be drawn into the scenario that the child creates; otherwise you're not the one in control. For example, the child might say, 'You can't make me do my homework, you're not my father.' The answer to this is, 'No, I'm not your father but that doesn't stop you doing your homework.' And ensure that both parents come at this kind of thing with the same approach.

It's not all about discipline

Use a little stick and a little carrot too. If the child continues to be rude, and oversteps the mark that you and your partner have agreed, punishment should be swift and decisive. Taking away their mobile phone or Xbox for a day will really hit home! But equally, if you pull a situation back from a potentially unpleasant scenario, and the child reacts positively, reward should be equally fast. Positive reinforcement is vital.

Children will respect you more if you are able to stay calm, and not lose control. If you're losing control then they're manipulating the situation and it will be increasingly hard for them to feel respect for you. Lay your rules, stick to them and pick your battles carefully. Sometimes it's okay to let things slide, sometimes not. But you don't want to be in a situation where it's a constant fight. Just make sure that when it slides, it's your choice, not theirs

Respecting children and their feelings and helping them adjust

Children aren't just nice pets that need biscuits and scratching behind the ears. They're people with feelings and a voice and they need to feel that sense of respect within a household. Listen to them, talk stuff through. Make sure they know that their feelings and opinions are important. You and your partner might be the ones that lay the basic ground rules for the household, but your children should have input.

Sitting together and having a 'house meeting' can do wonders for hearing everyone's concerns and desires, and ensures everyone has a say in how things run. But equally, one-to-one time and checking in with them all is important too.

All children are different and some children will adjust faster and better than others. Some children are gentle and reserved and will need treating more softly than those who are more open. Don't expect them all to fall into position in the same way, and ensure you look at each child involved as a separate person, with individual needs.

'All children are different and some children will adjust faster and better than others . . . Don't expect them all to fall into position in the same way, and ensure you look at each child involved as a separate person, with individual needs.'

Respecting the rules of your stepchildren's natural parents

Finally, when you and your partner draw up the boundaries for your new household, taking all the previous issues into consideration, give thought also to the other parent in each case. If you guys run your house one way and the children go to their other parent and it's completely different, this could be confusing and unsettling. If it's at all possible, try to find some common ground between all places so that the children experience a sense of continuity wherever possible

Of course that sounds easy in an ideal world and in a large number of cases, this is going to be impossible – whether there's animosity there, different family values or simply an incapable parent, the reasons for diversity are various and many. Work with what you've got, stand in the child's shoes if you can, and create the best solution you can with the tools at hand.

Summing Up

▨ Children are complicated and complex creatures, and will display a baffling array of actions and behaviour. The key to relating to them rests with your ability to listen to them, to hear what their needs are and act accordingly.

▨ Remember that children who are acting up are doing so for a reason. They may be feeling resentful, insecure, lost or angry. Staying calm and retaining control of situations will not only serve to produce a more positive result, but will also build trust between you and the child. If you lose the plot every time something goes wrong, that child is never going to respect or have faith in you.

▨ Getting to know them and not rushing things will really help. Children need time to adjust – in fact all human beings need time to adjust to new situations – and laying the foundations of trust and respect early on will pay off in the long run.

Chapter Three

Extended Family and Exes

Helping children remain close to the other parent's extended family

Once you have all set up home together; you, your partner and any children you have, it's perhaps tempting to feel like 'keeping it in the family'. You have your own home together, you and your partner may have parents still alive and kicking around, so there are grandparents, maybe aunts and uncles . . . there may be family occasions to plan, Christmases to spend together, even extended family Sunday roasts. But it's really important for the children to stay in touch with their other parent's family too.

The other parent may have siblings, parents, cousins of their own, perhaps even more children with a new partner, and it's really imperative that your stepchildren retain and develop relationships with their other extended family, as much as they do with your own. On the 'other side' there will be grandparents, aunts and uncles – maybe even half-brothers and sisters – who are your stepchildren's family, and the child should be free to enjoy loving relationships with them too. Talk to the children about the other family members too; show an interest so that you know who is who in their lives and their family. Making the child feel comfortable talking about their other extended family with you will help to make him or her feel less like there are two camps, and therefore torn between split loyalties.

Make sure you encourage this. Work with the other parent if possible to ensure Granny's birthday isn't forgotten, for example, and that the child sends a card if they're not seeing them. If access arrangements mean the child is supposed

'Making the child feel comfortable talking about their other extended family with you will help to make him or her feel less like there are two camps, and therefore torn between split loyalties.'

to be with you when the other parent is having a large family gathering, be flexible. This is not about your arrangements; this is about the children's family life.

High days and holidays

Christmas can be a real sticking point for blended families, with all parents naturally wanting to spend the festive season with their children, and perhaps sharing it with extended family. Remember again that it's about what's best for the children and be kind and flexible. Perhaps alternate the years, or take it in turns to do Christmas and New Year's Eve.

Think too about annual holidays. You might want to take the children away, or have time with grandparents during the summer holidays – but so might their other parent. Try to come to an amicable arrangement over time and access for holidays and family occasions.

However you work it out, remember to try and keep communication open, and don't feel hurt or resentful if your stepchildren don't take to their step-grandparents or step-aunts and uncles in the same way. As with your own relationship with them, they will develop a different connection and this will take time. It all takes time!

Deciding to have a new baby together

Deciding to add to your family by having another baby can raise all sorts of considerations. If you're making a conscious decision to try, it's probably a good idea to tell the existing children, as it will give them time to get used to the idea. You will have no idea how they're going to react, whether the baby is planned or not, but the best thing you can do is listen. Let them voice their feelings and try not to put them down if they're struggling to accept the idea. Reassure them, let them know they're still important to you and as with everything, just give it some time.

The idea will take a while to settle. It's best for the children's biological parent to be the one to break the news, before discussing it as a family. He or she can reassure them that they are still very much loved and it will be a more intimate moment for them as opposed to a 'family meeting', which will feel impersonal.

The children may well of course be excited by the idea, which will make it easier all round and means you can all start planning together, shopping for cots and choosing names. But it's also common for them to feel a rush of concern for the other biological parent. Don't leave it to the children to tell them. It is big news that could be upsetting and unsettling, and it's far too large a subject and responsibility for them. Exes should talk to exes about this kind of thing. Let them know what the plans are, make sure they know what's going on before the children visit them again. The last thing you want is for the children to get the third degree over this, particularly if they're not overjoyed by the news. Be prepared for some emotional fallout from the ex too – babies are an emotive subject.

Once the baby arrives, you will have a whole new set of issues as the children come to accept a new person in the house. As with normal siblings, there are issues of jealousy and rivalry for parents' time. Deal with it in the same way, offer love and time to the older children as much as possible and involve them in the new baby's life if you can. Encourage them to hold him or her, push the pram, help with the bath. Acceptance will depend to a certain extent on involvement.

Becoming a step-grandparent

Becoming a grandparent is an exciting adventure, and so is becoming a step-grandparent. Whilst both can be rewarding and fun, there is a difference in the way the relationships work. Grandparents will often feel it's easier to connect with their biological grandchildren, largely because their father or mother is their own son or daughter. There is a familial connection going back years and it's a relationship that has been there from the start – it's more familiar and requires less conscious effort. Grandparents may also feel more at ease when communicating with their biological grandchildren, for example being able to laughingly insist on a hug or a kiss when they arrive or leave. There are few barriers.

Developing a relationship with a step-grandchild can bring enormous rewards and has a bond all of its own. It's perhaps easier to develop this if you can start early, when the child is young, but it's never too late. Try not to rush things, but

'Developing a relationship with a step-grandchild can bring enormous rewards and has a bond all of its own.'

develop a new, separate relationship with your step-grandchildren, getting to know them, finding out how they work. Love and affection will grow as the relationship develops.

How the relationship grows will, to some extent, depend on the child's relationship with your own son or daughter. It's a good plan to let the immediate family settle into some kind of routine and level of acceptance first, and give them some space to all get used to each other. If your step-grandchild has a good relationship with your son or daughter first, it will be easier for them to grow to accept you too.

If you already have grandchildren of your own within the same family unit, there may be loyalty issues that arise, for both you and your grandchildren. And it's as well to acknowledge that you will never feel the same about your step-grandchildren as you do about your own. But as with step-parenting, even-handedness is vital, as is giving time to both your grandchildren and your step-grandchildren separately. They are not all from the same background and it's completely fine to realise that you can have a very different connection to them. But it is definitely important to give all of them your time and loving warmth.

Think too about what you'd like the children to call you – will they all call you Granny and Grandpa, or will the step-grandchildren call you something else? It might even be something you talk through with the children themselves, ask them what they'd like to call you. Their answer could also give you some great pointers in how the children view you, and therefore the grounds to start working on that relationship

If you don't have grandchildren of your own before acquiring step-grandchildren, this can be more of a challenge as it will be completely new territory. Don't be daunted! After all, you must have managed to raise at least one child before and grandchildren's needs are not so very different. Give them time, treat them with warmth and respect, get to know them and develop your own relationship with them. Invite them to spend time with you and make them feel included as part of the extended family.

It's also important to remember that you could be one of two, three or even four sets of grandparents that the children have in their lives, and for the children this can be overwhelming, daunting even. Bear this in mind when setting up your own relationship and try to give them the time and space they need for *all* their extended family!

Access and arrangements

Arrangements over access and residency can be a thorny subject, whether the separated parents get on okay or not. Reaching an agreement over time spent with the children and the level of responsibility each parent takes is often a complex process and can lead to conflict.

Firstly, it's important to remember who is at the centre of all this and keep the child in mind when making arrangements. It's important not to let conflict polarise the parents into two separate camps, making the child or children feel torn. Try not to let arguments and legal action rule the day if possible, but engage the other parent, try to talk plans through and set up routines. A set access routine works best, so that all parties know where the children will be and when. This is particularly important for the child, as children really need a sense of routine.

If the child is old enough, you could engage him or her in the process to a degree, perhaps they would like to have input as to how much time and when they want to be with each parent. But largely you should, with your ex-partner, be able to come to some arrangement over routine and residency that works for the children and is manageable for you both.

'Arrangements over access and residency can be a thorny subject, whether the separated parents get on okay or not.'

Negotiation and counselling

As with making any kind of contractual arrangement, there is negotiation. You will need to realise that you will probably have to make compromises, and that not everything is just going to go your way. It's about finding a mutually agreeable arrangement and you may have to give in to some things that you don't necessarily want. Keep in mind the bigger picture. And if it's impossible for you or your partner to reach an agreement without hostility, there are options before reaching for the lawyers.

Relate family counselling offers help for specific issues such as this and will work to find a solution without delving into any other subject. See the help list. Mediation can work very well too and offers the safety of being able to make arrangements 'without prejudice'. This means that what you agree during mediation cannot be held up in a court of law further down the line, and this freedom often enables two parents to make a better arrangement, without the fear of it being upheld legally. It's a more compassionate approach. The Children and Family Court Advisory and Support Service (Cafcass) is a service set up to support families that is independent of the courts, social services, education and health authorities and all similar agencies, it is a non-departmental body operating within the law set by parliament and under the rules and directions of the family courts. One of its primary purposes is to support when parents who are separating or divorcing can't agree on arrangements for their children. Contacting Cafcass would be a good place to start looking for mediation support. (See the help list for details.)

Dealing with a difficult or aggressive or violent ex-partner

As with making arrangements over access and residency, dealing with a difficult ex is challenging. It's complicated further if you believe your children to be in danger when they're with an ex. As a step-parent it's part of the job to be supportive if it's your partner who has the difficult ex, but equally there needs to be boundaries. You need to think about how to deal with issues such as the disruptive ex entering your home, for example, or what to do if the children are in danger. How it will affect the children. And how it might affect your own children too.

The issues with difficult ex-partners are too varied and detailed to cover here, but if mediation or counselling has failed, then your recourse is to take the legal route. Just ensure you keep an open dialogue with your children and stepchildren – balance what you discuss with them but try to avoid keeping them in the dark too much

Case study

I'm a step-parent and my husband's ex has consistently harassed us for years, using the children as collateral, and has issued constant legal action. We have custody of both children, who were removed from her years ago based on her and her new spouse's behaviour, which was aggressive and manipulative. She threatens me and my partner and has been violent towards us, until the eldest child, feeling responsible, went back to live with her of his own volition. The younger one now wants to join his brother, tempted by the ex's promises of material bribes and freedom to do what he likes. Not only are both children now completely disrupted and behaving badly, but we've been drawn into yet another legal wrangle, with the latest court filing indicating a claim on my home, which I purchased with my own assets before even meeting my partner! We are now faced with yet another bitter legal battle which does nothing for the serenity of our household, let alone the children's peace and safety. It's hard to know what to do in this situation.

With anything like this, it is of course paramount that you get good legal advice, but as for your home life, try not to let this affect your relationship with either your partner or the children. Offer the children a warm welcome, try to normalise things as much as possible and give them love without having to deal with the ex's situation. It's important for them to know you care about them, whatever happens. And realistically the same goes for your partner. It's not their fault their ex behaves like this. Make sure you communicate calmly over this and make sure also that there is time together without this matter being the sole subject of conversation. Set aside loving family time, otherwise it will end up taking over everything.

Your stepchild's relationship with their other parent

Whether or not the children were younger or older when their parents separated; regardless of whether or not the split was amicable and however much it might have been the 'right' decision, all children will grieve for the separation. Deep down all kids want their mum and dad to be together and have a 'normal' life, so whatever the circumstances were when they split up, they're going to mourn that loss.

Understanding this will help you to support your stepchildren in this. It might be hard to grasp, particularly if there have been years of rows, or the other parent is difficult or unfit. You might wonder why the child can't just see how much better it is for Mum and Dad to separate, or how much better off they are in their new situation. But it doesn't work like that for children, and helping them to bridge that gap, and try to maintain a healthy and loving relationship with their other parent is paramount in both their happiness, and therefore the related contentment in your own home. Never put them down for wanting to see their other parent, or wonder aloud what on earth they want to do it for. Be there for them if it's difficult and show love and understanding and do not take it personally if they struggle to accept you.

Best case scenario is that the child or children can enjoy a happy, healthy, loving relationship with both parents and a different, yet still loving and happy, relationship with any step-parents too. That's in an ideal world and of course in some cases will be impossible. But try to keep an open mind, remember that children love their parents, whatever happens and whatever they're like, and ensure you can be supportive and caring if it doesn't all run smoothly.

'Offer the children a warm welcome, try to normalise things as much as possible and give them love without having to deal with the ex's situation.'

Your partner's relationship with the ex

Tempting though it might often be to wish the ex would disappear in a puff of smoke, they're going to be around and you're also going to have to deal with the fact that your partner and his or her ex have a past together. There may be shared experiences that your stepchildren will have been involved in, holidays for example, and it might be hard sometimes not to feel like an outsider, particularly if your partner still has a good relationship with their ex. In fact, perversely, if they have a really good, open relationship this could even sometimes be harder than dealing with animosity and aggression. Don't let that green-eyed monster move in!

Try to remember that if everyone gets on, it can only work better for the children. Talk to your partner if you're finding it hard, and draw boundaries so that you can both understand how relations with the ex should be handled.

30

How do you feel if your partner spends time with his or her ex and their children together as a family still? Are you expected to invite the ex round and how would that feel? Make sure these concerns are all aired calmly and sensibly, before letting resentment or jealousies build up.

Helping stepchildren cope with the death of a natural parent

If you have stepchildren and they lose a natural parent, it's either going to be your partner or the parent they live with when they're not with you. It's a terrible thing for children to experience the death of a parent but you will need to be able to be there for them and support them

If it's your partner that dies, of course you're going to be doing your own grieving too and it's important that you recognise the loss both you and your stepchild or children are experiencing. It may mean that the children no longer live with you or stay with you, and this can be difficult for you both – try to ensure you still maintain contact with them if this happens

Children experiencing grief may display it in many different ways and the chances are it's not going to simply be a case of them feeling sad and crying. They may be angry, withdrawn, rebellious or difficult. Grief counselling can be a huge support at a time like this

Ensure you honour both the child's feelings and the memory of their parent. Don't give up talking about the one who has died – it may feel like you're being kinder by not mentioning it and, of course, no child needs it rammed down their throats when they're grieving, but remembering Mum or Dad in a gentle way is important.

Remember also that the child may have feelings of resentment towards you as a step-parent, and try not to take it personally. If you're their stepfather or mother and their natural parent has died, they may struggle even harder to accept you, mourning the loss of their biological parent and feeling resentment that they need to accept you instead.

Discussing and supporting your partner in their role as step-parent

It's important that you both know where you stand in your new roles as step-parents and what you expect from each other. Sit down and chat through how you both feel it will work. How much input do you expect the other to have with your children? How will you make access routines work? If one parent's child or children are at home full-time and the other parent's part-time, how will that balance out? Think about who is going to do the household chores like cooking and school runs – as you all come together as a family, now is the time to work out the nuts and bolts of who does what in the family unit. Setting this out now will help with potential resentment and misunderstanding later on.

'With time, patience, communication and love you can make it work. Just don't expect it to happen overnight!'

Think too about emotional issues. As a step-parent you will have a relationship with your stepchildren, but how far does that go? A very common response from stepchildren is 'You're not my Mum/Dad – I don't have to do what you say.' Think about how you'll cope with that, and other scenarios, and how you'll support your partner in situations like this. It's vital you work this kind of thing out together as chinks in the armour will really enable children to gain control.

Keeping expectations realistic

Even in that seemingly perfect traditional nuclear family structure where Mum and Dad are still happily together and they have two fantastic, well-behaved children there will be struggles and issues. So pulling together a stepfamily is definitely going to have its challenges. Making family life work is sometimes tough and you're very likely to find that there is a lot of effort and patience that needs to be put in. Don't be daunted. These things really take time and you should expect a bumpy ride – no family is without its quarrels and disputes. Your stepfamily will be no different, but with time, patience, communication and love you can make it work. Just don't expect it to happen overnight!

Summing Up

- There's a whole world of family considerations outside your four walls, in the shape of your stepchildren's natural family, grandparents, aunts and uncles. It's important for the children to have good relationships with all their family, including their stepfamily, but it's also good to understand that there are differences.

- Children will often be able to give step-grandparents and step-aunts and uncles a good indication of how they expect the relationship to work, simply in the behaviour or communication they display towards them.

- As the family changes and adapts, so too will all those involved. Be prepared to give it time and for the path to be anything less than smooth!

- It's often hard to find the balance with exes and partners alike but the more stability and open communication that can be fostered the better.

- Try to work with ex-partners to build a happy arrangement so that children can feel relaxed and not pressured to take sides, and try also not to take things personally.

- Remember too that your partner has chosen to be with you, not them, and be happy if they still manage to get along with their ex amicably. The opposite is very definitely much harder to work with.

Chapter Four

Accepting Change

Involving stepchildren in your living arrangements or wedding plans

A great way to enable stepchildren to accept your future plans as a new family is to try and involve them. If they feel like they're on some kind of roller coaster over which they have no control, they will struggle to feel safe and happy. However, if they feel they've got a say in how things work, they're more likely to be open to change.

Planning your living arrangements can offer all sorts of opportunities for involvement – from looking through the different accommodation options in the paper or with the estate agents, through to viewings and decisions over rooms and locations. Once the living space is chosen, there are 'house rules' to think about and work on together. Make sure *everyone* is involved though, not just your own children, or even just your stepchildren. It's easy sometimes to overcompensate, and it's vital, if you have any, that your own children do not feel left out.

Planning a wedding is a complex and time-consuming job. It can be fun and, again, offers plenty of opportunity for children to be involved. First off though, you need to let them know what's happening and wherever possible ensure that everyone is happy with the decision.

Opposition to those plans

It's entirely possible in many cases that there are going to be children – yours or your partner's, or both – who do not want a wedding, who are averse to the whole idea of you and your partner marrying; who may not even want to be at

'A great way to enable stepchildren to accept your future plans as a new family is to try and involve them.'

the wedding itself. It's important to find the balance here. The children need to understand that this is something you and your partner want to do for your future happiness and they will need to accept it, but equally you want them to feel happy about it. Let them talk about it, and listen to their concerns. The more you encourage them to voice their feelings, the better you can deal with them head on.

Whether they're happy about the plans or not, involving them can bring about a positive attitude towards the event. Viewing potential venues, looking at dresses or suits, choosing menus and the guest list . . . all these things can be done with the involvement of the children and will help to make them feel included and part of the new family.

Accepting your feelings as a step-parent – positive and negative

If you imagine that you're going to move forward into your new stepfamily without any hiccups or intense feelings of your own, think again. Taking on someone else's children is no easy task, particularly if they're a bit older, and you should take time to ensure you deal with your own feelings. You'll be busy making sure the children are happy, but make sure you take care of yourself too.

On the positive side, there is the absolute gift of being a parent, of being a part of a child's life and helping to form their development and giving them the tools to be able to go forward into life successfully. It's a rewarding, wonderful job and you're going to enjoy so much of what that has to offer.

Step-parents may put a lot of pressure on themselves to love and care for their stepchildren and then find that it's not as easy as they thought. It's important to understand that this is a different relationship than the one you have with your own children or your partner. Being a step-parent has a role all of its own and it's not healthy to give yourself a hard time if you find you don't love them the same way as you love your own for example, or struggle sometimes to feel kind towards them if they're being difficult.

'Being a step-parent has a role all of its own and it's not healthy to give yourself a hard time if you find you don't love them the same way as you love your own for example, or struggle sometimes to feel kind towards them if they're being difficult.'

Perhaps you might have feelings of resentment if you feel that your time with your partner is monopolised by them; or if you feel your partner takes their side in an argument. Perhaps you feel angry that the stepchild or children don't seem to take your parenting or discipline seriously. It's natural that you want to do the right thing for everyone concerned but that doesn't mean you won't have misgivings. It's not uncommon to have negative feelings towards your stepchildren – what is important is that you cut yourself some slack, and keep in mind that all relationships take time.

Accepting the change in your own life

Change is always a challenge, and coming together as a stepfamily is going to bring about big changes in your lives, for all of you, whether you have children of your own or not, whether the children are at home full-time or only at weekends. The partner you have had a relationship with is going to be your full-time, live-together 'spouse' and that means your relationship with them will change too. It's good to be aware of this change, and as far as possible, prepare yourself for it, but until you're actually in your new space it's going to be hard to judge what those changes will be and how you'll feel.

Keep a dialogue going. Remember to talk to your other half about stuff you're finding difficult, and be prepared to hear their concerns too – after all, it's a change for both of you. Making sure you are both talking openly and embracing the change together will enable you to support any children that come as part of the deal. It's an even bigger change for them in their short lives and they're going to need continued and consistent support from both parents to facilitate their acceptance of this massive upheaval.

The benefits of family counselling

Family counselling services such as Relate offer specific sessions for stepfamilies coming together, offering invaluable support where sometimes it's hard to work things through. Counselling can be simply to offer the family the tools to be able to get along together better, or for more specific issues, such as difficult teens, going on holiday as a family for the first time, problem behaviour or moving in together. See the help list for more information.

Whatever your issues, and you will have them, remember that nothing lasts forever, and that with time and love and patience, the emotional roller coaster will get easier to ride. Who knows, you might even enjoy it!

Children with special needs

A special word now for step-parents taking on children with special needs. As with taking on all stepchildren, there are challenges to face and hurdles to overcome, but this situation will call for a whole new outlook.

Be really clear about what you're taking on. It will of course depend on the child's needs, but look into how your day-to-day life will be affected and make sure both you, and any children you have, are fully prepared for it. It could mean the house has to be adapted, there could be behavioural issues. It could mean that one child in the house requires much, much more attention that the others and you need to identify how you will deal with that. It will also of course affect the relationship between your and your partner. Where one partner will have been living with the situation on a daily basis, the other will have had the opportunity to go home at the end of the day. How will it feel when you are all in the same house together?

Most of all, consider how this will affect your own children. How much will their lives change and how much of your time will be taken away from them. Ensure you really look at this carefully before taking it on. You can have a fully rewarding relationship with a child who has any kind of special needs, from autism through to physical disability, but it will change your lives. Communication is vital here to understand fully the changes, and ensure children know what is coming and how it will be handled

Summing Up

- When two families come together, whatever the structure, there will be some real ups and downs as everyone settles into their new role.

- Family counselling can really help if anyone is struggling to cope, but do keep in mind the need to keep talking to each other.

- Make time to listen to each other's concerns and be prepared for strong feelings of your own – positive and negative.

- Just remember these things change and grow all the time and with time, the rollercoaster should level out a bit. Nothing lasts forever!

Chapter Five
Day-to-Day Life

Being organised and developing routines and house rules

House rules don't necessarily just refer to a rota about household tasks and chores. Think of it more as a kind of charter, describing what each of you expects from the family unit as a whole

The charter can cover everything from outlining the way the stepfamily members react to each other, to setting up family routines. Listening respectfully to each other, dealing calmly or in a set way with conflicts and discipline, ensuring that you make time for each other or even setting aside a day for family activities can be covered, as can pocket money allowances and time curfews, and how time for TV, computer games and eating together is divided. It's vital that everyone has input into this to ensure they all know the rules, and have had a say in how they're set up. It's also a good way to prevent the loophole: 'Oh, I didn't know we had to do that.'!

Make it a point to sit down regularly and review or discuss how the charter works and yes, why not include household chores in this charter too. If there are a lot of you it's unfair that any one person – usually Mum or Dad – should end up running around doing everything. Engaging everyone in simple tasks such as taking turns to empty the dishwasher or hanging out a basket of laundry will really help.

Make sure you set time aside for fun too. Maybe Sunday could be the day you all do something together for example, and it's also important, if not every day then at least when it's possible, for the family to sit and eat together. It's really important that you enjoy quality time together and there's an old saying, 'The family that eats together, stays together'. There's a lot of truth in that.

'It's really important that you enjoy quality time together.'

Sometimes it's the only time a family actually gets to talk to each other properly, find out what's going on in their lives and keep up with their interests. Turn off the TV, sit down together and enjoy each other's company.

Combining household traditions in all households

Where your children or stepchildren have other parents it's safe to assume that there will be differences in the way the two households are run, and this could throw up some issues. Perhaps the children will have less order or an easier ride at the other house and come home feeling resentful that they have to engage and be helpful in your home. 'Why should I? I don't have to do it at Mum/Dad's house,' might be a familiar cry. The opposite could be true of course, with the other parent being much stricter than you and your partner. Whatever it is, it's hard for children to adjust and you will need to allow a little time for settling back in as the children go back and forth each time.

Try not to get drawn into comparing the two. If it's not a viable option to discuss this with the other parent to try and create some similarities between the way the two houses are run and how the children are expected to behave, the only thing you can do is maintain the status quo at your place. Rather than responding to them by criticising their other parent's system, respond by acknowledging the difference but letting them know that it doesn't affect the way things are run at your home. 'I know that's what Mum/Dad does, but when you're here, we do it this way,' is a good approach. Don't judge the other parent; just carry on with your own thing.

It's possible too, of course, that your partner will have a very different outlook to you on how the household is run. The same outlook perhaps as their ex-partner, and this could be challenging! In the same way that negotiating with your partner's ex over the children will require patience and compromise, so too will this. Talk it through with your partner, identify key areas that you have differences in and try to work out some middle ground. Do this early on; don't let differences fester and become resentments later on.

Growing as a family

Building a happy family unit within the bounds of all relationships

Establishing trust is vital in creating a strong future for you all as a stepfamily. Learning to work with each other, to communicate clearly and for children to feel safe takes time and practice, but continuity and kindness are the cornerstones of this process.

Understand that a stepfamily is not the same as a biological family. When two families are blended, the variations in the setup can be diverse, and flexibility is essential to creating a happy family situation. It's not going to be the same as a traditional family – the children will have other parents and spend time away, you may well have different family values to your partner and therefore the children will be used to different rules. There may be conflict with ex-partners or children who find it hard to accept the change; maybe one of you doesn't have children of your own or you have children with vastly different age ranges. Whatever the situation, it's important to approach it all with an open mind. Trying to make it all fit into your idea of a perfect family isn't going to work.

Don't take stuff personally. If the children are difficult with you, it's highly likely that it's because they're sad, or afraid, or missing their other parent, or feeling guilty. Don't let it get to you – try to remember what it's like to be young and unsure, and offer a warm response. Be wary of overcompensating too. It's not uncommon for a step-parent to feel the need to support their stepchild or children and sometimes overdo it, overlooking their own in the process. Include everyone and be even-handed wherever possible, allowing time for the whole family. And make sure you set aside special time for your own children. It's perfectly acceptable for you to give them one-to-one time away from everyone else. They will need that time with you

Having the right to discipline stepchildren takes time too, and building a relationship first is important. Developing trust and respect before starting to exercise any kind of influence will make that authority more effective and acceptable. A calm approach and the capacity to listen to them will pay dividends.

'Developing trust and respect before starting to exercise any kind of influence will make that authority more effective and acceptable.'

Going on holiday together

There are a few things in life that are recognised as having a very high stress factor, such as Christmas season, moving house and divorce. And also on that list is going on holiday! It might sound daft, but this kind of intense time together can offer serious challenges. You will probably be spending more time all together than you do normally; you're all likely to be staying in a smaller place than you're used to, without all the things you have at home. Then there is the actual travelling itself, which can be utter hell sometimes, particularly with small children. Delays at airports, traffic jams and travel stress generally can be a huge pressure. It's also true to say that if there are simmering resentments or issues with any family, the intensity of a holiday together is likely to bring them to the surface. Plan ahead! Develop your holiday survival plan before you set off and be aware of adjusting your expectations.

Firstly, as a stepfamily you should expect a stepfamily dynamic. It's important to do things together, but it's also important to understand that children will want to spend time separately with their biological parent, and this is fine. Make a plan before heading out, setting aside family time and time with your children. Forcing everyone to do everything all together all of the time is unlikely to bring you the results you want. Again, compromise is key, and having a plan for the time you're away will give everyone some kind of structure. Think about what you'll do in the days ahead and you'll save a lot of boredom and uncertainty affecting the younger members of the family. Think too about sleeping arrangements, access to bathrooms and cupboard space, and make a plan for the day of arrival, so that everyone has something to look forward to. This can help with the tedium of the journey too.

For the travel part, again have a plan. Think about things you can take that can offer distraction if there are delays, whether it's colouring books or handheld games. Pack snacks and drinks, and a packet of wet wipes.

Be aware too that as you're away, the children may miss their other parent or feel guilty about being away from them with their new stepfamily. Help them to work through this without taking it personally if you find them pining for the parent back at home. Sending them a postcard or buying them a gift will help, and for younger children, perhaps planning for this beforehand by suggesting they bring something of Mum or Dad's with them can help too. Transitional objects can really help to bridge that gap and make the child feel connected whilst away. If the child wants to, establish a way for them to communicate with their parent at home – perhaps an email or Skype session. But be aware of finding a balance – you want the child to enjoy their time away so beware of this communication taking over too much of your time. It's important for children to know it's okay to feel like that and be able to say so without upsetting anyone else though.

Your own relationship

In amongst all this, don't forget how you came to be in the situation in the first place. Yes that's right, your partner! The one you loved so much you decided to set up home together? That person is still very much there and you need to nurture that relationship just as much as you need to consider the needs of the children. If your relationship becomes about nothing more than working through family matters, running the house and paying the bills, romance will fly out of the window!

Make time for each other. Ensure that at the end of the day when it's just the two of you that you commit to spending some of that time together, talking, being close. Flopping straight down in front of the TV will feel tempting, but how about giving yourselves half an hour at least to connect before you switch it on? And maybe you have stuff to talk about that relates to the family or the children, but it's also good to try and get away from that. Talk to each other, about your day, about other things. Remember you're not just parents. You're lovers.

Go on a date every now and again. Get a babysitter booked, put on something nice and go out for dinner or to see a show or film. Keeping this kind of romance alive in your relationship is really important. It's also good for the children to see a happy, healthy relationship between the pair of you, not just a frazzled, worn out set of parents. You're a role model for their lives and displaying a happy, loving relationship is setting a good example.

Summing Up

- Growing as a family and stepfamily will need lots of time, and lots of communication.

- Make sure everyone has a voice in family decisions, and work to try and build continuity in all the homes the children live in.

- Don't neglect your own romantic relationship with your partner in the process of settling the family and children into stability and routine.

- Be conscious that whilst being even-handed with the children is vital, spending quality time separately with your biological children is also vital.

Chapter Six

Money!

CSA or child maintenance and how to manage it

When two people separate and there are children involved, it's common for some kind of financial arrangement to be set up to support the primary carer; i.e. the person the child or children spend most of their time with, which in most cases is often still the mother.

Child maintenance is important to ensure that the children are supported and should be used towards a child's everyday living costs. Separated parents can make an arrangement themselves and where possible this is desirable, although talking about money with an ex is often difficult. If possible, try to work it out taking into consideration what the children need, and how much is reasonable based on the income of the one paying the maintenance. There is little point in draining them completely so that money is unbearably tight for them, as this will make it difficult for the children when they visit. But an amicable settlement out of court will make for a happier situation all round and therefore calmer circumstances for the children.

'Child maintenance is important to ensure that the children are supported and should be used towards a child's everyday living costs.'

Mediation and negotiation

If it's something that you're struggling to come to a satisfactory arrangement over, there are options for mediation, where a third, objective person will help negotiations, or perhaps the CSA (Child Support Agency) or courts can be involved, which will then become a more legally-binding and formal arrangement. Directgov or the child maintenance teams can offer guidance and support with this and contact details can be found at the back of this book.

Keeping the children out of it

Remember that when talking about money, it's not something the children should be party to. Resist grumbling out loud if someone is not paying maintenance if possible; make sure children aren't drawn into an uncomfortable situation.

Arguments over money can make children feel split between two camps. Where it might be frustrating if financial situations are unresolved, and perhaps you may find you're even having to pay for your stepchildren as their other parent refuses to support financially, remember that this is potentially part and parcel of becoming a new family. Shoulder this and avoid sounding your resentment in front of the children. It's not their fault in any way, shape or form, and they should not have to take on feelings of guilt or defensiveness.

Ensuring agreements on expenditure in the household

Sorting financial matters out with an ex is one thing, but coming together in a new household brings its own challenges. There will be joint expenditure and there may be a large difference in what each of you are bringing in. As single parents before moving in together you may be in receipt of benefits such as Tax Credits, Housing Benefit and so on, and these will definitely be affected as you become a joint income household.

Before moving in together, do look at how your income is going to be affected and work out how you'll make it fit. On the HMRC website there is a tool to check how your Tax Credits will be affected for example, and most local authorities will be able to tell you how any benefits you are receiving will be reduced or changed. Details for this site are at the end of this book.

However you work it out, it's really vital you both know where you're going to stand once you move in. You don't want to get off on the wrong footing by finding suddenly that your income drops without you expecting it, or that perhaps where you thought there was a kind of financial balance in your incomes, that one of you is suddenly a lot worse off. If you plan these things, look at them carefully and make sure you know the score before taking the plunge, then the transition will be all the smoother. Identify how you'll support each other and how you'll feel if one of you is the main breadwinner for example.

Budgeting for a larger family

Once you've all come together as a family, even if there is only an increase of one or two in the household that you've been used to, you'll really notice the difference financially. Most families would agree that the biggest and most consistent cost in a larger family household is the food bill. Children can consume an alarming amount of food in a week!

Clothing too will be expensive, and as you come together as a bigger family it's likely you've got a larger house, with perhaps bigger fuel bills or greater rent or mortgage repayments.

Whilst it's true to say that overall your bills will increase, it's also possible that there may be two of you contributing to the budget. Whether this means you'll be better or worse off will depend on each couple's own personal circumstances. But try to sit down and look at this together, perhaps when you're going through your joint income and so on, so that you can create an effective income and expenditure plan together.

For shared household costs it might be a good idea to set up a joint bank account, with what you each pay into the account directly related to your income. This can be used for things like paying the rent or mortgage, fuel bills, the big weekly shop, car costs, school uniforms and so on.

'Once you've all come together as a family, even if there is only an increase of one or two in the household that you've been used to, you'll really notice the difference financially.'

School trips, activities and holidays

Occasional expenses such as school trips and holidays can really creep up and bite you if you don't plan for them. Christmas too. It's not uncommon for families to pay for things like holidays and Christmas presents on a credit card but then spend ages paying them off, with lots of interest. It's far better if you can plan for such eventualities and save for them.

Think also about school trips. Many schools offer children exciting opportunities such as a skiing trip, so try to plan for those if you think you might be saying yes! Think about the cost of it coming up, and consider also how that kind of experience will make the other children in the house feel. If it's something they're going to get to do in a couple of years when they reach the same point at school then it's fair to tell them they have to wait their turn. But if you have stepchildren who may be in another school that doesn't offer such an opportunity, then it's perhaps a good idea to look at creating a treat for them too. Even-handedness with all your children is vital.

As with your joint expenditure, a savings account is a great idea for setting up a holiday 'piggy bank'. Even if you can't always pay regularly into it. If you've got a kitty before booking and setting off it'll make the whole experience less stressful; and less expensive, without all those interest repayments.

Pocket money and budgeting for children's needs

Finally, look at the costs of the children, including their pocket money. Work out how you're going to handle their pocket money – will they all have the same or will it increase as they get older? Will they have to earn their money or will you just give it to them? Try to ensure that the children understand the approach to pocket money and if there has been a big difference in how stepchildren have received pocket money before all coming together, you'll need to sit down with a plan to ensure it's levelled out between them all.

Children can be really expensive, from the cost of food bills to the possible strain of school fees. *The Guardian* reported in 2012 that the average cost of raising a child had reached £218,000. But there are many additional expenses you will need to build in. Extracurricular interests such as dance classes or horse riding lessons, kung fu classes or even just lifts here and there can really add to the cost of bringing them up, so be aware of the lurking costs and try to ensure, again, that if you're shelling out a lot for one child for a certain thing, that you find a way to balance it with the others. Seeing one child receive expensive support for a hobby whilst the others receive nothing will definitely lead to resentment.

Looking after the future

Saving for university

Children can fund themselves through university, choosing to support themselves with part-time work, students loans and so on but many families feel this will distract them from their studies and want to support the child financially.

If your child or children want to go to university it's as well to start planning for that as soon as possible – at 2012 the average cost for completing a degree stands at around £50,000. Many students are leaving university with enormous student loan debts and parents, step-parents and extended family will often want to support children seeking this kind of future.

Yet another savings account? Well yes, it's probably a good idea. If you have a good income, set up a monthly standing order to simply pay a set amount in each month. Shop around for good interest rates so that you can help to increase the nest egg. And do ask other family members to help if you can. Grandparents will often be supportive in this instance.

And finally, consider whether you will give your child an allowance whilst they're at uni. Fees and living accommodation will account for the biggest cost, but they also need to eat! Think about how this will work and make sure you take into consideration all of your children. If you have lots between the two of you and they might all want to go to uni, you need to be prepared financially!

Changing your will

Death and taxes are the only certain things in life, so make sure you get your will in order. You might want to change it to reflect your new circumstances – particularly if you're only living together. Perhaps one or both of you might still even be married to your exes, in which case you could die and they could inherit your money! Think about how you will divide your money and assets between yourselves and/or your children and stepchildren too. And make sure you do it together at the same time. There are lots of online services to support you with making a will but for guidance check out the government website Directgov for advice. (See the help list.)

Summing Up

- Making financial arrangements can be fraught and frustrating but it's important to keep children out of it.

- Pay attention to the changes that your cohabitation or marital situation will have on any benefits and think too about the potential increase in your household bills.

- Make sure all children understand how things like pocket money and financial support for hobbies will work out, so that there is little room for resentment.

- Planning for the future, as with any family, will be important. So think about wills, university costs and the cost of setting your children and stepchildren up for a secure future.

Chapter Seven

Advice for Step-Parents

The challenges of being a stepfather

Often, stepfathers shoulder a lot of responsibility – both financially and emotionally – but may feel unappreciated, separate or powerless within the family unit. Even in these enlightened times, it's still very often the case that the man is the main breadwinner so he may spend less time at home being part of the family – and as mothers are still more likely to end up being the primary carer, his ex may well have custody of their kids, meaning he could find he spends more time with his stepchildren than he does his own. This can lead to feelings of guilt and resentment.

The father who is more present in his children's lives will face different challenges. He may be a stay-at-home dad, and struggle to be accepted at the school gates by the daunting army of mums. This can mean he might lack that network of 'mum' support that can be so helpful to parents – with picking up kids or sharing school runs, or just simply socialising with other parents at the school and sharing parenting tips and experiences. This can make a tough job even tougher!

Whatever your family set-up, making sure you have family time together is important. Perhaps ensure that you all sit down together at the end of the day and have dinner together – if not every night then at least sometimes – and set aside time at the weekends for fun together. You want to build relationships with your children and stepchildren and it's hard to do that if you or your partner are never there.

'Often, stepfathers shoulder a lot of responsibility – both financially and emotionally – but may feel unappreciated, separate or powerless within the family unit.'

Quality time with all your children

If you are spending more time with your stepchildren than your own, make special time for yours when they're with you, as they're bound to be feeling it too. Ensuring that you spend time with your own children when they're there is vital, but be sure to create some family time with everyone together as well, otherwise you'll end up with a chasm between your children and your partner's. And as if that wasn't enough to think about . . . trying to balance time with your own children and time all together is hard enough, but just to add to the level of input, it's also important to try and get to know your stepchildren too, and build a separate relationship with them. It's something of a juggling act!

As a father and a stepfather you can be a positive role model and it's important to engage the children in fun and healthy activities. Do 'Dad' things with them like going camping, or going on bike rides or swimming. Give them time without Mum and make sure that you're not just the bloke who comes home at the end of every day knackered!

Forming a bond with a stepdaughter

A father/daughter relationship is a wonderful thing, and there is no reason why you shouldn't have a strong relationship with your stepdaughter in a similar way. Having positive male role models in her life is not only important in terms of offering balance, but equally she will use those role models as something to benchmark her choices in boyfriends and friends further down the line. As a stepfather you have a responsibility to give her a good male example – typically to be strong but caring and communicative.

If you have stepdaughters living with you, the chances are high that your partner, their mother, has custody of them and you may find that both you and they are struggling to accept that they see more of you than their own father. Don't let this fester unsaid, talk to the girls about this, letting them know that you will never try to take their father's place, but that you care about them and you're there to be their stepfather.

It might be tempting to assume that having boys is easier for men, that they can share playing football, or building rockets or fixing cars – but there's absolutely no reason why stepfathers can't encourage girls to do this kind of thing too. Equally, a good parent will always try to take an interest in their children or stepchildren's hobbies and pastimes, so if you have to get on your knees and play with My Little Pony, you should do it.

The first man a girl ever loves is likely to be her dad, but a stepfather can often come a close second. There is a special bond that can exist between stepfathers and daughters, and like all these things it will take a bit of work. It might be easier when the girls are younger, and as they mature into teens and older, it will perhaps be harder to find a level of communication. But maintaining a loving and present warmth in their life is important throughout. Even grown up girls need hugs from their dads – and stepdads!

Respecting her relationship with her mother

Most mothers will be concerned about the new man in their daughter's life, and it's vital that you try and put your stepdaughter's natural mother at ease. The fact that her mother is also your partner should not stop you identifying that she too will have those concerns. Are you a suitable role model for her daughter? Will you treat her with respect? As a man, will you be able to meet her needs as a step-parent? All these questions and more, possibly even more serious ones about safety and protection will all be in her head and you need to reassure her. Let her know that you respect her daughter, talk things through with her and keep her involved. You can build a rewarding and worthwhile relationship with your stepdaughter, but remember that mothers can be lionesses when safeguarding their young – and this will be particularly so for girls!

'The first man a girl ever loves is likely to be her dad, but a stepfather can often come a close second.'

Forming a bond with a stepson

As with having stepdaughters, stepfathers face similar challenges with stepsons, inasmuch as they are perhaps likely to spend more time with you than their own father, and you are responsible for being a positive role for them. It's just as vital that you offer a good role model for boys – as they grow up they will learn from you and take on much of what you teach by example. Make sure that example is a good one!

Spending fun time with a stepson might be easier on the face of it, but you need to look for common ground. As with girls, engage in things you know he enjoys and make time to spend together doing things you both like. Although there's a good chance it's going to be the case, don't just assume because he's a boy that he'll automatically be into cars, guns and sports, find out, get to know him. Be wary of straying into his own father's territory though. If he plays weekend football, for example, check that it's ok before turning up to cheer him on. His natural father might feel that you've encroached on his space, and your stepson might feel uncomfortable. Learn to strike a balance and never let the child feel torn or suffer split loyalties

Respecting his relationship with his natural father

Finding a balance for your stepson between yourself and his natural father without making him feel guilty is important. Men and boys have a more economical use of conversation than women and girls, so maybe talking things through with him in great detail and depth might not be what's needed. But equally, he needs to know that you're there for him, but as a stepdad, not a replacement. Spend time on a one-to-one basis, ask him about his own dad, keep it open and light. Let him know that it's fine for him to be proud and excited about things he does and shares with his own father and that it's OK to talk about those things with you.

The challenges of being a stepmother

At the heart of a family it's often the mother who runs things. Whether or not she's working, it's much more often the case that she'll have responsibility for the day-to-day routines, shopping, picking up and dropping off children, organising afterschool clubs, even the adults' social calendar. Women are naturally efficient organisers and can sometimes seem to juggle an endless stream of tasks! Does this sound like you?

Because of this, your stepchildren may feel sometimes that they're bossed around by you. You're the rule-maker, the one seemingly always telling them to do this, that and the other. Taking on someone else's children can be overwhelming, daunting even, and it will be hard not to feel undervalued if you find yourself in this situation, but remember – you don't have to do it all. Draw on your partner's strength and time to be involved in the running of the house and the children and you'll probably find it runs a lot more smoothly!

It's a big responsibility, being a stepmother – both to boys and girls – but there are parts of being a stepmother to a girl that are more demanding. You're a role model for her as well as a parent, and by teaming up with her father, you're showing her that love and new relationships in blended families can work. Girls can be notoriously niggly and catty and you can find yourself on the end of that. As stepmother to a boy, you're also giving him another female role model but in a different way. How he views you will have a bearing on how he views women when he grows up

Forming a bond with a stepdaughter

Stepdaughters and stepmothers can often have a difficult relationship. There may be jealousies there, hormonal or emotional clashes; a huge thing to consider is the child's protective feelings towards her own mother. Her mother may have been able to separate from her father okay, but finding her daughter spending time with another woman, a stepmother, will often be more threatening and difficult for her than anything else. If she's making that clear at home in front of her daughter, that daughter is going to struggle not to feel disloyal when she's with you. Girls may pick up on this emotional stuff more than boys.

It might be that you develop an easy relationship with your stepdaughter, falling into a comfortable sisterhood without too much hassle, sharing time and space with ease. But being realistic, it's unlikely. Building a bond with your stepdaughter, like everything else, will take time, but doing things together that you both enjoy, trying not to get drawn into petty arguments or jealousies, talking things through together – all this will help. Get to know her on her own, go shopping or swimming together perhaps. If it's really difficult to get along, find a moment where it's not so bad, call a truce and draw up a charter together outlining what kind of behaviour you'd like from each other.

If it gets really difficult, ask her father to step in. If you're both rowing with each other and you're not sure how to resolve it, perhaps he can mediate. If it's simply a case of your stepdaughter behaving badly, ask him to have a quiet word with her, explain that it's hurtful and unhelpful and see if they can find a way for everyone to feel happier together. He may even be able to talk to his ex and sift through the emotional strife behind it. Bad behaviour can simply be a case of growing up of course, in which case you're just going to have to ride it out!

Respecting her relationship with her own mother

'It can be hard to get it right and develop your own relationship with your stepdaughter – one that doesn't threaten what she has with her mother.'

A girl's relationship with her mother can be such a special connection – shared experiences and love of the same things, genetic similarities and a close bond – all of these things are natural and desirable between a mother and her daughter.

Being stepmum in all this can be a difficult task. It can be hard to get it right and develop your own relationship with your stepdaughter – one that doesn't threaten what she has with her mother but that is also close and caring. Just offer a warm welcome to your stepdaughter, and if you need to, explain that you will never try to take her mother's place. As stepmum you can have a lovely, sharing relationship with her but you need to guard against taking it personally if she is guarded, or confrontational.

Remember – as with your relationship with your stepdaughter, her mother is always going to be there too and you have to find a way to all get along and ensure the happiness of the child.

Forming a bond with a stepson

You might think it's going to be harder to develop a relationship with a stepson, but it's just playing with a different set of cards. Boys usually have different needs and different interests to girls – although there are exceptions to every case, of course – so you just need to look at what those needs and interests are and work with them

Boys also have just as much need for love and warmth as girls do. When they reach a certain age, hugging and kissing will be strongly discouraged! But that doesn't necessarily mean they don't need attention and affection. You'll just need to find another way of doing it

Spend time with your stepson alone, show an interest in what he does. You're not his mum but you're also a role model for him and how he sees you will affect how he sees women in later life. Show him kindness, warmth and love. And of course patience. Lots and lots of patience!

Don't be a 'wicked stepmother'!

If you're like a huge amount of women these days, the chances are you're running a house, parenting your own children and your stepchildren, you might well also be working and let's not forget trying to have some kind of loving relationship with your partner in all of this! It would be understandable if you seemed to find yourself most of the time rushing around, barking orders at the kids and not having a moment to breathe.

Stop! It's really important first of all that you give some time to yourself, or you'll go nuts. Secondly, you need to set aside time for your family. Avoid being the nagging stepmother who does nothing but hustle kids and make dinner and wash clothes and work hard, by allowing time for fun. And yes, you can make that time. Diarize it if you have to! But make time.

All relationships take work, and your relationship with your stepchildren is no different. Out of all step-relationships, the relationship between stepmother and stepdaughter could be the one that has the most potential for arguments, frictions, jealousies and petty fallouts. With girls, you could both feel rivalry for the man you love – her father and your partner – but equally of course with boys you could struggle to find common ground, a way to communicate with each other. It will all just take input. Spend time finding out about your stepchildren, give of yourself. You can build a warm and loving relationship but it won't happen if the most you say to them in a day is, 'Pick up your clothes from the bedroom floor' and, 'What do you want for dinner?'

Summing Up

- Stepfathers have an important role to play in their stepchildren's lives – offering a chance to give them a positive outlook and a sound male role model.

- How you react to each child doesn't just relate to what sex they are, but their personalities and their individual needs overall. Remember to keep in mind the relationship your stepchildren have in place with their natural parents and respect and encourage that.

- Nobody will tell you being a stepmother is easy, and it isn't. But we can take a lot of the challenges we've talked about in the first part of the chapter and turn them around – some of these things are absolutely what make it worthwhile.

- Building a relationship, being a sound role model, teaching them to communicate, accept changes in relationships – all of these things can have a positive impact on your stepdaughter's life and future and if you do a good job, the rewards can be countless.

Chapter Eight

The Dreaded Teens!

Changing times and understanding teenagers as they grow

Parents who have been through the teenage zone with their offspring would understand this, but when children hit their teens, they can often turn into a completely unrecognisable person. 'He/She changed into a monster overnight' is a phrase you've probably heard other people use, and there's no doubt about it. As children hit their teens, everything can change. Your gentle, sweet pre-teen could turn into a snarling, disobedient rebel. A normally chatty, friendly child can suddenly disappear into the depths of their bedroom, only grunting occasionally and coming out for mealtimes.

Facing teens can be difficult, not just for parents but for the children too. They'll be battling with a big physical and mental change, as their bodies prepare for adulthood, and they start to detach from parents, mentally and emotionally. It's another key stage for physical growth and change and your teenager will need more sleep – so much about the child you know will change, it's hard sometimes to keep up.

'As children hit their teens, everything can change. Your gentle, sweet pre-teen could turn into a snarling, disobedient rebel.'

Caught between being a child and an adult

As your teenager grows and develops, it becomes increasingly hard to bridge that gap between adulthood and childhood. Actually, your child fits into neither camp for a while and the transition can be tough – for both them and their parents and step-parents. They don't want to do the same things any more; they don't need the same input from their parents.

They want to be adults, but they often still feel like children. Recognise this paradox and work with it – think of it as having your child on a bit of elastic. Sometimes they'll stretch it taut as they strain to grow up, other times they'll want to ping back and be close and cared for again, but through all of that, they absolutely need to know you're holding the other end of that elastic.

Needing space

As they hit this important developmental stage, teenagers won't need the kind of micro-management that children require, and they will be keen to be making their own decisions. They'll also want to spend less time with the family unit, often preferring time alone or time with their friends, and this withdrawal can be difficult. It might feel that your stepchild only ever grunts at you when they want food or money, but this process is all part of learning to detach from the safety of parenting. It's a really important factor in the process of maturing.

Explain to your teen that you respect their need for space and perhaps pledge to try and give it to them without grumbling! But demand something in return. Stress that when they do converse with you or your partner, their siblings, step-siblings or other family and friends, they show some respect and make the effort to be pleasant. They might need time and space away to get used to growing up, but equally, they can make the effort to be civil and respectful and display reasonable social skills.

Hormones

Ah yes, good old hormones. As your child hits their teenage years, hormones rocket wildly around their bodies, causing behavioural changes that both you and the teenager will struggle to adapt to. Mood swings and crazy emotions can take everyone by surprise and it's probably wise to accept that this is going to be tough on everyone – particularly the teenager. They may be shaken by how intense their emotions can feel and they will struggle to know how to cope with them. Dealing with this is going to be a roller coaster, for sure. But it will pass. Hang on in there!

Rebellion, confrontation and disobedience

Coping with a teenager requires the patience of a saint! Raging hormones, fluctuating emotions, straining at the leash for more independence and an overall detachment from parental responsibility makes for a difficult time, for both teenager and parents. But sometimes this behaviour can spill into an unacceptable zone.

Teenagers can be rude, rebellious and moody, and whilst it's valuable to understand the emotional and hormonal flux they're experiencing, it's also important to establish house rules. Teenage tantrums can upset everyone, drain emotional resources and even teach younger siblings or step-siblings bad habits. You absolutely need to impose some level of respect and reasonable behaviour.

Children tend to accept that parents know best, and even if they grumble, will accept the discipline or authority dished out to them. Teenagers, on the other hand, will question every single thing that comes out of an adult's mouth, will argue black is white and will unquestionably know much better than Mum or Dad or any kind of step-parent. This can be tiring and lead to frustration and argument. Reasoned argument to some degree is worth a go, but you are far better using some kind of bartering system (reward scheme!) or by meting out discipline by taking away something that is important to them.

If they're rude and storm out refusing to listen or communicate, how about cutting their mobile phone off for a bit? Disobedience or a refusal to come out of their room and stop playing computer games could see that computer put in a safe place until a truce and new game plan is put in place. You don't need to shout and get cross, arguments like that are futile. But if the teenager is still living in your house and you're still paying the bills, you've got some control at least. Establishing consequences for their actions, good and bad, is vital to the development of their independence.

If your child is completely out of control, it might be a symptom of something greater bothering them, and a visit to your GP would be a good idea. There will be a support network that you can investigate, such as counselling. Whilst a certain level of rebellion in teenagers is healthy and expected, if the behaviour is beyond the bounds of acceptable, you need to look carefully at the options for dealing with it and your doctor is a good place to start.

Arguments and violence

Don't get drawn into heated rows if you can help it. You're far better to just keep quiet and maybe even leave the subject to approach calmly later on to discuss in more detail. And don't ever, ever get drawn into a violent confrontation with a teen. Keep your head and deal with it when the moment has passed – containing it if possible, but not retaliating, and certainly not leading with your fists. What will that teach them as they grow up? Violence is not the way to settle matters.

Teenagers will often be angry and aggressive – it's a good idea to encourage them to voice their anger in positive ways. Give voice to their feelings and let them express their emotions. And find outlets for that anger and aggression. Exercise and sport is a good way to let off steam, and team sports are particularly good for social integration.

Common ground and shared interests – ways to reach out

It will probably feel like there's an impassable chasm between you and your teen sometimes, but there are ways of reaching out. Respecting their growing need for independence is important, but equally you can't just drop them like a hot brick. They still need input from you and actually, whether they grumble about it or not, they still need to know that you want them around, that you want to spend time with them.

As teens, stepchildren can feel particularly on the outside, so make an effort to draw them in if possible. Find common interests and activities that you know they'll like. Make them feel involved in the house and family processes. Sports activities, going to theme parks, days shopping with girls – look at what they're interested in and find a balance between supporting those interests and doing stuff all together as a family.

'As teens, stepchildren can feel particularly on the outside, so make an effort to draw them in if possible. Find common interests and activities that you know they'll like.'

Helping teenagers to adjust to a new family background

The joining of two households is often fraught with difficulties, whatever the ages of the children. And teenage years can be turbulent without the emotional and physical upheaval of having a new home and new family. Put the two together and you're guaranteed some fireworks!

It might feel harder at times when faced with their teenage moodiness and rebellion, but helping teenagers adjust to a new stepfamily requires much the same kind of response as when they're any other age. They need communication, they need to be involved and they need to feel love and warmth. They need to know that their natural parents still have the place in their lives they've always had and they need to grow and develop their relationship with their step-parents slowly, building up trust and familiarity. You'll need to give them a bit more space and you really need to remember not to take it personally if it takes a long time for them to adjust and accept you as a step-parent. Have patience, it will take time.

As with all children, disciplining your stepchildren when they are teenagers should be something that you only do once the relationship has been built up. It's also important to identify that teens won't respond well to being told off, or issued instructions. They will respond much better to reasoned discussion, and establishing consequences in the form of punishment rather than wagging a finger will have a far better result.

Involving them in household decisions as young adults

It's really common for parents and step-parents, struggling to adapt to the change in their child, to recognise that change and react to them appropriately. A teenager will want more of a voice, not only in the things that affect him or her, but perhaps equally in the way matters are run at home. It's important to listen to the voice of your changing child, to respect that, as a young adult, they may have valuable input.

'As with all children, disciplining your stepchildren when they are teenagers should be something that you only do once the relationship has been built up.'

A great way to show respect for the teenager as they grow is to involve them increasingly in household decisions. Not just that, but decisions that have a direct impact on their own lives. Negotiation over arrangements, and the building of trust over sticking to those arrangements, can offer a valuable opportunity for supporting their journey into adulthood. This could include decisions on a wide range of subjects including what they're allowed to wear, the curfews imposed and what places they're allowed to go to, keeping their room in a reasonable state, and whether they have to come to family events or on holidays.

Remember that as this is negotiation you have leverage to put in place the option for your teenager to earn rights too. Good behaviour could earn them extra time out, or chores around the house could earn them money. Engage them in this kind of reward programme and include their input into how this is set up. If they feel involved in the creative process, they're more likely to stick to it or employ it to their advantage. This will not only act as an incentive to be a useful member of the household, it will also give them a sense of self-worth. Earning stuff makes kids feel good.

Teenagers and younger stepsiblings

Brothers and sisters often fight like cats and dogs, whether they're biological relations or not. And when a child hits their teenage years it's likely they'll struggle even more to relate to their younger siblings or step-siblings. You may even find that children who have played happily together for years no longer get along, with the elder child withdrawing from the younger, leading to feelings of confusion, abandonment and sadness. The younger one will find it hard to understand why their elder sibling doesn't want to play with them anymore.

Talk to both of them and highlight this. Ask for understanding for both of them and be clear about what's going on. Your younger children or stepchildren need to know it's not about them, that their older relative is going through some changes and that whilst they won't last forever, they are growing up. And you need to talk to your teen and show them how the younger one is feeling. Try to establish a kind of truce based on understanding and awareness. Establish ways to encourage contact and closeness through these changes. Eating together is still a great way for everyone to check in together, for example. Don't let everyone drift apart, however sulky the response might be!

Summing Up

- Teenagers bring a whole new set of experiences as they start to change and mature, and having teenage stepchildren in the house, however often, can be a real challenge.

- Respect their growing need for privacy, and give them the space they need to process what's going on for them. But at the same time, make sure you continue to include them, to make them feel part of the family and to show them warmth and love. It won't last forever, and they will come back out of the other side. Just make sure you're with them along the way, however rough it is.

Chapter Nine

Sharing Parenting

Allowing your partner to discipline your child

We've talked in chapter 2 about respect and disrespect from stepchildren, and the best way to approach discipline with your stepchildren. But how will you feel when it's your child? However much you love someone, it's not always easy to allow them to discipline your children, and how the discipline is handled in your house is something you should talk about early on. It's hard for children to respond well to a telling off from people they don't love and respect, so during the early days it's a good idea to take things slowly. Building up trust and a warm relationship first is very important – if your partner steams straight in there, reprimanding them and laying down the rules, they're going to resent him or her immediately and you'll struggle to come back from that.

Talk to your partner about what you expect of your children in terms of behaviour, how they communicate and behave both with each other and with adults, whether they're expected to do chores, their routines for school and homework and so on, and discuss with your partner how the discipline is normally carried out when the children don't do what they're supposed to. If there are bigger issues it's better for you as the biological parent to deal with those, certainly in the early days, and mete out the discipline; but once a rapport is reached with the child or children, day-to-day stuff like making sure the children stick to routines can be well within the bounds of acceptable responsibility for a step-parent.

Make sure that you both know what is okay and what is not okay when it comes to discipline and ensure you present a united front. Let your partner know what you find acceptable and be clear about the boundaries. Children are arch-manipulators and if they sense you and your partner are not quite in agreement over anything, they'll find a way to use that! If you disagree over the

'However much you love someone, it's not always easy to allow them to discipline your children and how the discipline is handled in your house is something you should talk about early on.'

way anything has been handled, it's far better to discuss that afterwards, away from the children. Don't take their side in front of your partner. You'll undermine him or her and the children will lose respect.

Understanding the challenges a stepchild faces

Aside from the whole aspect of a new family, new step-parent and new living space, a stepchild faces all sorts of day-to-day challenges. Everyday routines and habits will be changed, and children will struggle to adapt to this. There could be new house rules, more children to share time and space with, a new school even. Merging the habits of two different households presents a fair few challenges and it's a good idea to recognise that. Try to aim for some level of continuity in shared routines and find some common ground in the way house rules are created.

Watch out for emotional strain or upheaval too. Children may be grieving for the parting of their biological parents, recognising that they won't get back together and mourning that loss. Facing that eventuality could mean seeing the step-parent as the one to blame – thinking 'Mum and Dad would be together if it weren't for you.' Jealousy for the new step-parent as the child feels his or her parent 'taken away' from them is also common, as is a refusal to accept the step-parent's authority.

It's the answer for so many of these issues, but again this will just take time. Reassure the children, bear in mind what an upheaval it must feel to them. After all, you have had years and lots of practice at new things and new arrangements, but in their short lives, this will feel enormous. Lots of love and lots of making them feel safe. Listen to them and never brush aside their concerns

Good communication is vital for all family members

They say it's good to talk, and this couldn't be more true than when dealing with families and stepfamilies. Communication is a two-way thing and it's vital that everyone not only gets to have their say, but also learns to listen to others.

Encouraging children to have a voice in household matters is important, but aside from this it's also essential to encourage them to practise the art of conversation. To be able to talk to others and listen too, feel confident about being able to say what they think, and respond to peers and adults alike with clear and reasoned dialogue.

Remember that with communication and listening should come respect. Learning to disagree without arguing is a useful skill and it's good to instill this in all household members; the ability to recognise a difference in opinion and accept it without having to win the argument.

A great way to ensure the family all get to communicate together is to eat together, without the TV or other distractions, and actually talk to each other. Find out what you all did in the day, make a point of doing this at least a few times each week. And set aside a regular time, perhaps once a week, to all sit down together and chat through family stuff – make sure relations are open and that children and adults alike are free to say what is on their mind without getting shot down in flames!

Parenting children who don't live with you

It can be hard to develop a sense of stability and inclusion if there is a child who is only with you for short visits and lives mostly with his or her other parent. It can be particularly hard if there are other children living with you full-time, as the non-residential child will often feel like an outsider.

Make sure that the child has a space that's all their own – their own bedroom if possible or certainly their own bed. Ensure that when they come they're made to feel part of the family, encouraged to join in with the other kids and make sure they keep plenty of their own 'stuff' at yours. Clothing, toys, books etc. – all this will help to make them feel part of the family.

Exercising discipline and rules over a non-custodial child is hard when they're not there very often, so you'll need to try and work with the child a bit on this. Let them know how things work at your place but be prepared to give them a bit of leeway – if they spend 80-90% of their time doing things one way, it's hard for them to accept the differences. I say hard, because it's not impossible

'It can be hard to develop a sense of stability and inclusion if there is a child who is only with you for short visits and lives mostly with his or her other parent.'

and children are more than capable of adapting to two lots of rules. But gentle guidance is the key here. Ruling with a rod of iron will make visits miserable for everyone.

Consider it's also possible that the ex – particularly if there has been an acrimonious split – may be giving your partner and/or you a less than glowing image at the other house. Try not to get drawn into that but understand if the child struggles to accept you, or is unhappy when he or she visits. Just try to give a warm and open welcome and hope that as the child grows older and can form more independent opinions, this will pass

Developing a relationship with the school

As a step-parent you may well find yourself collecting your stepchild or children from school and, dependent on the kind of relationship your partner and their ex have, you may even be involved in the child's schooling. How far your involvement with their school goes will depend on the situation with your partner's ex.

It's normal for the child's biological parents to have responsibility for schooling – from choosing where they go, to relationships with teachers and involvement in educational options. It's not usual for a step-parent to be involved in that, unless perhaps there is joint parental responsibility or maybe if the child's ex is unfit or absent.

As well as the school, think too about how you will handle school plays or parents' evenings. Who will attend these and how will the child feel about it? Talk it through with the other parent if possible, and the child too. For the child, having his or her biological parents involved and present for these events is of primary consideration. But it may be that step-parents would like to be involved, and the children may well want them included too

If yours or your partner's children are going to be attending a new school as a result of you starting a new stepfamily together, then it's important for the teachers to meet all parents involved. Teachers will benefit from knowing who is in the child's family background and they are well accustomed to knowing how to deal with blended or diverse family structures.

Summing Up

- The most important things to keep in mind when working together to form a successful and happy stepfamily are communication and collaboration.

- As step-parents, it's vital that you offer continuity as a unit and that all game plans and rules, wherever possible, are established before there are repercussions or a need to implement any kind of discipline.

- Make sure you're both coming from the same place and that you have acceptable ways of running the family that you set up together and agree on.

- Work out how things are going to run, identify what each of you expects from the other in terms of parenting your own and your partner's children.

- Decide what you expect from the children too – how you expect them to behave, to address you, to act around the house – and ensure that these rules apply to everyone.

- Talking to each other and finding calm solutions are key factors in ensuring a warm and happy communication for all family members. But most of all, remember that the most important thing is to ensure the safety and happiness for all children.

- Make sure you and your partner are on the same team, and if you disagree with each other over any issues, don't do it in front of the children. Talk quietly about it together later and decide on a common solution.

Top Tips for Step-parents

Get to know the children

Apart from the time you spend with them and their biological parent, get to know them separately and build a separate relationship.

Remember that children will be a permanent part of your lives

If the going gets tough, you've got to stick it out. You can't just duck and run if it gets difficult.

Remember it takes time

Rome wasn't built in a day and neither will your stepfamily be!

Work closely with your partner

Whatever the issues, whether it's a family fun day choice or house rules, make sure that you both come at it from the same angle. A united front will give the children security and ensure you maintain control. And if you disagree with each other, don't do it in front of the children. Talk it over later.

Spend time with your own offspring

Whether it's your kids or your partner's, it's vital that children get to spend quality time with their biological parents. Ensure you make time for this and embrace it without resentment.

Accept your stepchildren

They might not be what you would have chosen, and it could be a challenging relationship. But they are who they are and getting to know them, rather than trying to change them, will work far better.

Spend time with your partner

Make sure you keep romance alive despite all the family stuff going on around you!

Keep the gritty stuff away from the kids

Children don't need to hear gripes and grumbles about money and custody battles. Try and shield them from this as much as possible. Be grown up – you have no business being selfish, childish or self-centred as a parent.

How important is it?

Before launching into full-scale war over something, ask yourself how important it really is. With children and stepchildren, it's worth knowing when to pick your battles. Pick wisely.

Keep communication open

Talk, talk and talk some more. Listen too. Everyone should have a voice in your house and everyone else should be able to hear it and respect it. Make sure that it's a safe and considerate space for everyone to be able to communicate in

One set of rules for all

Whilst you need to acknowledge the difference in your relationship between your child and your stepchild, it's vital that within the family, all children are guided by the same rules and given the same privileges.

Help List

Al Anon and Alateen

Run along the 12 Steps of AA, this is the support group for families and friends of alcoholics.
Incorporating Alateen for younger members from the age of 12, it can be invaluable for children whose parents or step-parents are alcoholics or if there is alcoholism in the family.
Tel: 020 7403 0888
www.al-anonuk.org.uk

Be StepWise

Be StepWise is an organisation set up for those who bring children from previous relationships to their new family. It is a team of qualified, experienced professionals who have great empathy with step-parenting and stepfamily life.
Tel: 020 8761 1633
www.bestepwise.co.uk

Cafcass (Children and Family Court Advisory Support Service)

Cafcass looks after the interests of children involved in family proceedings. They work with children and their families, and then advise the courts on what they consider to be in the best interests of individual children.
Tel: 0844 353 3350
www.cafcass.gov.uk

Care for the Family

Care for the Family is a national charity which aims to promote strong family life and to help those who face family difficulties.
Tel: 029 2081 0800
www.careforthefamily.org.uk

DirectGov

Public services all in one place – a one-stop shop for all legal and government matters relating to parenting, child support and family support networks.
www.direct.gov.uk/parents

HMRC Tax Credits

Check what you are entitled to as a stepfamily, whether you're working or not.
www.hmrc.gov.uk/taxcredits

Institute of Family Therapy

The Institute of Family Therapy is the largest family therapy organisation in the UK. It provides high-quality training and clinical work in the field of systemic psychotherapy with families, couples and individuals.
www.ift.org.uk/

Parentline

Parentline is a confidential service free from landlines and most mobiles. You can call free for information, advice, guidance and support on any aspect of parenting and family life.
Tel: 0808 800 2222
www.familylives.org.uk

Relate

Relate offers family counselling and workshops throughout the UK and will have an office near you.
They offer specific support for families and stepfamilies. Your nearest office can be found through their website or by calling the national phone line.
Tel: 0300 100 1234
www.relateforparents.org.uk

Triple P Positive Parenting Program

Triple P parenting courses are available worldwide. Head office is based in Australia. For your local Triple P practitioner please go to the website.
www.triplep.net

Need - 2 - Know

Available Titles Include ...

Allergies A Parent's Guide
ISBN 978-1-86144-064-8 £8.99

Autism A Parent's Guide
ISBN 978-1-86144-069-3 £8.99

Blood Pressure The Essential Guide
ISBN 978-1-86144-067-9 £8.99

Dyslexia and Other Learning Difficulties
A Parent's Guide ISBN 978-1-86144-042-6 £8.99

Bullying A Parent's Guide
ISBN 978-1-86144-044-0 £8.99

Epilepsy The Essential Guide
ISBN 978-1-86144-063-1 £8.99

Your First Pregnancy The Essential Guide
ISBN 978-1-86144-066-2 £8.99

Gap Years The Essential Guide
ISBN 978-1-86144-079-2 £8.99

Secondary School A Parent's Guide
ISBN 978-1-86144-093-8 £9.99

Primary School A Parent's Guide
ISBN 978-1-86144-088-4 £9.99

Applying to University The Essential Guide
ISBN 978-1-86144-052-5 £8.99

ADHD The Essential Guide
ISBN 978-1-86144-060-0 £8.99

Student Cookbook – Healthy Eating The Essential Guide
ISBN 978-1-86144-069-3 £8.99

Multiple Sclerosis The Essential Guide
ISBN 978-1-86144-086-0 £8.99

Coeliac Disease The Essential Guide
ISBN 978-1-86144-087-7 £9.99

Special Educational Needs A Parent's Guide
ISBN 978-1-86144-116-4 £9.99

The Pill An Essential Guide
ISBN 978-1-86144-058-7 £8.99

University A Survival Guide
ISBN 978-1-86144-072-3 £8.99

View the full range at **www.need2knowbooks.co.uk**.
To order our titles call **01733 898103**, email **sales@ n2kbooks.com** or visit the website. Selected ebooks available online.

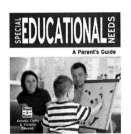  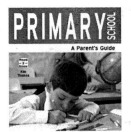  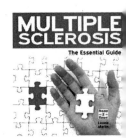

Need - 2 - Know, Remus House, Coltsfoot Drive, Peterborough, PE2 9BF